Boy Dad, Short Memoirs From a Father of Young Boys

G.T. DIGUE

Published by G.T. DIGUE, 2019.

BOY DAD
Short memoirs from a father of young boys
First Edition
ISBN: 978-1-7338687-0-9
Printed in USA

Table of Contents

To my wife,
        Thank you for supporting me in all that I do.
              To my boys,
    Without you guys this book would not be possible.

BOY DAD

Short memoirs from a father of young boys

INTRODUCTION

My name is George. I'm a husband, father, brother, son, nephew, grandson, cousin, and a friend. Well, I guess I am many things. I definitely always try my hardest to be the best at all my titles as I can be, even though sometimes it might seem being the best at all these things might not actually be what I am best at, at all. This book is about exactly that "wanting to be the best but feeling you might not always be, and accepting it."

This book is by no means in any way meant to be any kind of parent blueprint or rulebook. Children do not come with a manual, and I assure you I'd never try to write one either. Everyone parents differently, and as long as we all parent with love and good intentions with the best in mind for our children I believe we are doing it right.

Camden is 7, Conner is 5, and Cohen is 1 month old. Having 3 boys can be a bit challenging at times but for the most part a blast. Camden is in first grade. He loves to read, draw, and play every sport, and he is really good at all of it. Conner is 5. He likes playing sports, watching internet kid videos, and playing video games. The kid is absolutely obsessed with video games. He is a rock star at any game he plays. Then there is Cohen. He just turned 1 month. He is so sweet. Typical infant sleeps, poops, pees, and cries. He is healthy and happy.

This book is more of a journal. A journal of my life as some of these rolls I play while trying to be the best I can. In this book I will allow you to see my life as a father of 3 young boys through my point of view, and tell you about our family experiences and how we deal with them. I am definitely not a psychologist or any other type of doctor. I'm just an average guy living what we feel like is a normal life.

I'll have suggestions and answers to what has and hasn't worked for me and my family with all kinds of day to day experiences. Do I deal with them properly and rather I wish I have done things differently? I do realize no one is perfect. My goal is to help other parents look back at my experiences and realize that as well. I would be lying to you if I told you I have never felt defeated. We are parents, no one ever said it would be easy.

In this book you will also read about some of the toys we buy, the vacations we have had, even some of our favorite and not so favorite restaurants. I hope you can laugh sometimes and maybe even cry (hopefully not too often cry). Mostly, I hope you can learn from my personal experiences as a new father and realize, even if we are not in this together, WE ARE NOT ALONE! So please sit back and help me enjoy this ride we call life.

Chapter 1
Not Routine

It's all routine, right? Absolutely not! I am going to tell you about an emergency c-section and why it is not even close to routine. I will tell you how not only was it one of the most confusing moments of my life, but the most fearful moment as well.

Our first 2 boys were both born natural. With Camden it could not have been more natural unless we had him at home. The Mama was absolutely amazing she did not want any medicine and no epidural. Nothing, just her own strength and will power. She did so awesome.

Of course, I was surprised and extremely confused because people say labor and delivery is so hard and painful and takes a toll on a women's body. The Mama did not show any of that. Seriously, no screaming like in the movies, no yelling at me, and never screaming she hates me. Nothing. She was calm, but I could see she was in pain. She was silent and focused on her breathing. Or so it appeared anyway...

Don't get me wrong there were some moments which were extremely intense. I had never been so nervous my entire life. I guess with me having zero knowledge of any medical terminology other than what I had forgot immediately from helping her study, I knew nothing. It might have been better for me that way.

We went back and forth to the hospital multiple times before she was in actual labor. This was our first pregnancy, we really did not know what to expect. We did take the Lamaze classes so a lot of the things we were experiencing seemed not as scary. Just until... she went from 0 to complete in just 10 minutes! The monitors were reading odd saying his D-cells kept dropping.? D-cells? What's a d-cell???? Something to do with his heart rate...

This is when I could see some uneasiness in her face. The nurses pace picked up a lot and more people came into the room. They had The Mama change positions so many times. They told her to push! The doctor said, "If you can't get him out on the next contraction, we are taking him cesarean!" The next contraction came and her determination and strength from whatever she had left all came down to that last push. He was out! He was born! Why wasn't he crying? A few seconds later and... tears and screaming. Tears from him, tears from her, and tears from me. It was the greatest sound I've ever heard in my entire life up until that point.

Things were very similar with our next pregnancy. Conner, baby Nonn as Camden would eventually call him because Camden was only 16 months old when we brought him home. No-one probably would have thought it would stick, but that's his nickname now and he answers to it. He knows his name is Conner now, but when he was little, he might have thought it was Nonn or Nonna.

Some of the similar things with our pregnancy with Conner were things like not a lot of morning sickness (at least from my memory). The Mama was still upbeat, had energy, and no mood swings. We spent a lot of false alarms at the hospital with this pregnancy as well.

This pregnancy was however, a bit different because she had gestational diabetes this time which went away after her delivery. She did not require medicine because it was diet controlled. She has always eaten pretty healthy anyway, but now she was on a diabetic diet and had to check her sugar regularly. Finding out about the gestational diabetes was done with a test her OB/GYN gave her called a glucose test. They check her sugar then make her drink a small bottle of sugar water, then in one hour she has her sugar checked again. The results came back. She had failed. No biggy at this point, this just means she has to now take another glucose test, but this time its 3 hours long and her sugars are checked every hour to see how her body breaks down the sugar. She failed this test too, which means she now has to monitor her sugars and control her diet.

Other than this big difference most of this pregnancy seemed the same. Due to the gestational diabetes the doctor did not want to allow her to go past the due date so we scheduled an induction. The induction is a process where the doctor inserts the Cervidil into the cervix to help it to soften and dilate. This is what looked to me like a pill with a string attached. She had an epidural as well with this labor along with the Cervidil. I am pretty sure she accepted the epidural this time due to the contractions being so intense. After a little time passed the nurse hung Pitocin in an IV bag. It is a synthetic hormone her body already produces to induce labor and also help with getting her cervix to soften. "Pitocin is no joke," her words not mine. Her contractions we could tell were super painful this time. Way worse than with her first labor. About 10 or 12 hours later he was ready to arrive. The Mama's doctor was still on his way so she waited to push. Probably about 10 minutes had past, then her doctor arrived and before we knew it, he was here. Baby Conner has made his debut to the world screaming and crying. Again, he was crying, The Mama was crying, and so was I. Another healthy baby boy.

On to our third pregnancy...

We already had two boys. The pregnancy, labor, delivery, and recovery all went well in my opinion. There were some nerve-racking moments but we were prepared for this pregnancy, or so we thought...

This pregnancy started out a lot differently than the other two with morning sickness and cravings. Though the morning sickness was not just in the mornings we should call it the all-day sickness. This one started out so differently that we thought, "Oh wow maybe we are having a girl." After everything she ate no matter if we cooked it or we went out to eat, maybe an hour later I could have bet she would say, "That didn't sit well with me." It was seriously after everything she ate. This pregnancy she also had gestational diabetes and it was also diet controlled. Toward the end of the pregnancy we set up an induction date should she not go into labor on her own. The date fell on a Friday. She started having contractions about 3 minutes apart on the Wednesday before. Ironically enough her doctor was due back from his vacation at 5 p.m. that day. We arrived at the hospital about 3 p.m. and at about 4:30 p.m. they wanted to discharge us. We asked if we could wait for her doctor. The hospital called him and he said to admit us.

At this point we are pretty excited. We gathered our stuff and headed to our room where we planned on having the baby. We started getting comfortable telling jokes and watching television. Later, the on-call doctor comes in the room because of some changes on the monitor.

He decides to break her water. He used a tool that looked like a thin white stick. A few nurses are in the room with us while he does this. After a few minutes everyone is gone, then the heart monitor starts doing something funny. We figured the baby was just moving so it could not get a good heart rate. The nurse comes in and looks at the monitor and has The Mama move on to her knees and then...

This is when everything goes from "normal" to "what in the world is happening." The nurse was pretty calm, as she should be; after all, she had told us she has been a nurse in labor and delivery for over 40 years. She asked The Mama if she would press her call button. After the call button was pushed and someone answered the nurse said calmly " I need some help in here please." There must have been a code somewhere in that statement because within seconds there were about 6 nurses and the doctor who broke her water in the room.

At this point The Mama and I are both a bit lost as to what is happening. Everyone is calm and each person seemed to have a different job. No one told anyone what had to be done it was just getting done. I think The Mama was way more in tune with the situation because she asked the doctor what the process was for a c-section. He briefly and when I say briefly, I mean in about a 20-word clip note version told her the process. He has a nurse get him something else to monitor his heart rate better it also looked like a stick but it was supposed to go inside her and next to the baby to get a more accurate reading than from the bands around her belly. He had to check for something first I really don't know what he was looking for but he felt something... then he says, "prolapsed cord." One of the nurses asked if he was sure he shook his head and said with a defeated look on his face, "Yes." At this point, confusion has definitely set in on us. Neither of us knew what this meant. The Mama started to tell the doctor and nurses she was scared. "I'm scared guys, I'm really scared?" The doctor told us a prolapse cord is when the cord comes out before the baby.

Every time the baby would start to come into the birth canal, he would pinch his cord. A nurse then switched the doctor places and put her hand in place in order to what I assume was to stop the baby from pinching his cord. The nurse was on her knees at the foot of the bed then they wheeled my pregnant wife and the nurse with her hand holding our baby in, out of the room straight into surgery for an emergency c-section.

Let me back up a bit. I told you how they were going to use another way to monitor his heart rate. It was something I have not seen before. I forgot to mention with one of the other boys they stuck what looked like white stick in her, and attached a tiny hook into the skin on his head and it monitors his heartrate better. The stick the doctor was going to use for Cohen looked similar but worked differently. Remember I told you The Mama said she was scared? Well this is when on the inside I completely lost it. I was a wreck on the inside. She is after all the strongest person I've ever met and she is scared and I'm supposed to be her protector and I cannot do anything but sit back and watch all this going on with complete confusion. A sense of helplessness filled my entire body, I was lost. All I could do was stand there in our room staring at the door that they just rushed my pregnant wife out of. Half of my world was just rushed into a surgery room. Staring at that doorway all I could see on repeat in my head was all of those people taking her away. After about 5 minutes or so which seemed like eternity, I walked to the nurse's station and only 1 nurse was there. I automatically assumed that all the other nurses were in surgery with The Mama. As soon as the nurse saw me, she said, "Are you dad?" I said yes. She said she would go into the surgical room to seem if she could get an update and for me to head back to our room, and she would be there in a couple of minutes.

I went back and not too long after the nurse who traded the doctor places on the bed came in and said "He is a pretty loud screamer. Baby is perfect and they are finishing up with Mom now." I was able to see Cohen in the recovery room before The Mama had arrived. He was beautiful just absolutely perfect. It was super exciting to see him finally. I was so relieved to see him and know he was safe and healthy.

As wonderful as it was to finally see him, my nerves were still going wild. The Mama is still not back. I do have this beautiful perfect baby in my arms, so why am I still falling apart inside? Why is she still not back? Time slowed down for me so much, minutes seemed like hours. I prayed so hard from the time we arrived at the hospital, and now even more, it was the only thing I could do to keep from having a breakdown. The Mama truly is my best friend. People call their spouse their other half. She is more than half. She is my 51%, because she has my whole heart too. My stress level had probably been about a 10 out of 10. The nurses and doctor said she was doing fine and would be in the recovery room soon but I could not calm my nerves until I could see her for myself.

Soon after probably 30 minutes or so. The surgeons wheeled The Mama in on the bed. She was a bit drowsy still and when I asked if she was in any pain. She just nodded her head. She had no epidural so the meds they had given her were working their best I'm sure, but she was still very uncomfortable. I brought the baby to her face so she could see him, and at that moment it seemed that all of the pain she was in and would have to go through was worth it. Let me be the first to say this was probably the scariest day of my entire life.

In many cases a c-section is scheduled at some point throughout a pregnancy for many different reasons. Our first two boys being born naturally gave us no reason to think Cohen would be any different. I'm sure The Mama had an idea as to what all the possible outcomes could be. As for me though I knew the possibility was there but since we never discussed it, I never gave a c-section too much thought. All we wanted was another happy healthy baby.

The doctors and nurses did a super job they knew exactly what to do. Nothing seemed to worry them at all. They were definitely trained and well prepared for anything at a moment's notice. As for The Mama and I though we definitely were not prepared for what happened. We always knew it could be a possibility for anyone, but we did not have any idea it would happen with us. Everything worked out well with both The Mama and baby Cohen. She had a lot of pain for a while, but she is so strong, so recovery seemed fast for such a major surgery. The c-section was not planned or scheduled so for us it was definitely **NOT ROUTINE!**

Chapter 2
Play ball!

A lot of parents think they know everything about their kids. Do they really though? Some kids are really open and some are not. I always thought I was one of those parents who knew my boys and everything about them, after all they are not even 10 years old yet. It's easy to assume that everything is perfect in their lives, they are super happy, and they do not have any problems. Sure, I would have always thought, "Problems? What kinds of problems can a 5 and 6-year-old have?"

Definitely as a father of 3 boys I would love to assume that every day is amazing for all of them. I pray that they are always happy and try to eliminate any worries. I always thought any worries they might have would be a bad thunderstorm, scary dragons, or zombies coming to attack. My life as a kid I mostly remember fun times in the summer swimming, playing in the woods, or sledding in the winter and jumping in leaves in the fall. I believe that being a kid should be just that. Being a kid should be fun, worry free, and playing till they pass out at bed time.

Here was the reality check for me. All that super fun no worries stuff is only while the kids are really little, until they are about 4 years old when they start having neighbor friends or going to preschool. It really is quite heartbreaking when you actually find out this beautiful perfect world you thought you have created is not as perfect as you thought.

We started Camden in coach pitch baseball when he was 4. Of course, no one actually believes the kids will play or want to do anything besides bat. Let's face it, just because I believe that baseball is the greatest sport ever invented, "THE GREAT AMERICAN PASS TIME," to a 4-year-old it's a pretty boring game. I really think that coach pitch and t-ball are mostly for the parents. It's a great time to finally meet other parents after 4 years of trying to figure out where all of our spare time went. There are plenty of great laughs from watching the cute kid running the wrong way down the bases or laughing at the kids picking dandelions in the outfield. It truly is a great time for all parents.

When we would come home Camden would always want to bat more. The Mama and I would stand in the front yard and toss him the ball a bunch of times to let him hit it. He was just having a great time batting not realizing he was practicing. The concentration he had was amazing for his age I thought. He came to a point where he was getting really good and hitting the balls really hard. His focus with batting did not allow a whole lot of time for conversation since he was trying so hard to hit the ball so far. We definitely had a lot of fun always too. We made our own games and own rules that usually only I had to follow. As he got better and even stronger, we eventually had to stop batting in the front yard. We worked on throwing the balls back and forth a lot. After he had about 10 strikes or so we would have him throw all the balls back. His accuracy and strength of throwing became very good that first summer.

Eventually, Conner took notice to our games we would play as he became older and he started to enjoy playing as well. Conner started out as Camden did with not being able to make contact with the ball unless we tossed the ball directly at the bat. Watching them both have so much fun while learning Daddy's favorite sport was so wonderful for me. I learned a lot myself those first summers. I learned Camden had great speed and strength, and learned Conner was ambidextrous. It was surprisingly extremely difficult for me to teach him how to throw and bat left handed. Eventually, Conner would hit too far to be able to bat in the front yard as well.

In our house we all love baseball I have a favorite team, but still watch any baseball that is on the television. Just because we could no longer bat did not stop us from playing catch. At times The Mama, the boys, and myself would all play catch. It still to this day is such a great time. We laugh and give each other tips. We like to see how high we can throw and on plenty of occasions I would have to chase the ball into the street.

We would play a lot of catch with the football at times as well. This was definitely a learning experience for me since I have never had a whole lot of interest in football. My boys would be surprised to know how many tips I received from friends at work about how I should catch a football. Kicking is still something I'm working on. These boys are very impressive with how good they have become so quickly. Either they are really good, or I'm just that bad. Probably a little bit of both.

Playing catch with the four of us is always fun. Playing catch one on one is when things start to get personal. I am not talking about on a competitive level, I am talking about getting into their minds. The concentration eventually was not so intense the more they practiced. This was nice because this became time for the boys to really open up. They would have silly conversations a lot of times, but so many times we would have serious conversations.

We would talk about the what if questions. The "What if we could throw the ball to heaven for Peepaw?" To math questions. "What is a million plus a million?" We even talked a lot about zombies. One day I asked Camden what day it was and he told me the day and the date. He was only in preschool at the time but he caught me so off guard with the date too, I will never forget. Talk about a proud Daddy moment. Of course, these are all conversations we all would expect from a child 5 or 6 years old. Some of the conversations we have are some very unexpected conversations. These are the kinds of conversations I'd never expect, the ones that would show me the perfect, safe, worry free world I thought I have created for my children, was not at all as I hoped it was.

Truth is, kids have a great way of hiding their feelings and secrets. Maybe its fear of talking about it, or maybe they just don't know how to deal with it at all. These are the times I found out who the bad kids or bullies were in the class. What things about school they don't like and what makes them nervous. What kids in the neighborhood are doing or what their brother has been saying or doing and getting away with.

Without the boys even knowing it they are really relieving their own stresses by talking about them. I was able to help them talk about what has been going on and ease them of stress. Stress that to an adult would not matter; such as, why he was not able to be a line leader 2 days in a row or when he can be the light captain next even.

I always hoped that I could keep my boys in a perfect world. I hoped I could keep them in a giant stress-free bubble. I guess up until this point I had forgotten even kids have stress, even kids think, and even kids worry about real life. Just because the things they stress about seem super small we have to remember, they too are also super small. Small problems in a small world seem like huge problems to small people. After all, this tiny world they live in is what is making them who they will be one day as adults. We will be surprised to learn some of the things we do learn from them. We are their heroes, the adults who they look up to. Small advice for a small person in a small world, sometimes is a big relief. So, if you think you know everything about your kids there is another way to help you to learn more, **PLAY BALL!**

Chapter 3
Not My Kid!

For a long time, I always thought my kids were so good. They are the most well-behaved kids I know. They are boys, and boys can be crazy and do wild things at times, but they are pretty good. I guess I have officially experienced firsthand the old saying, "boys will be boys." My guys do sometimes find themselves getting into some unfavorable situations I'd say.

Camden seems to always find the "bad kids" to play with. He knows he is not allowed to do certain things such as swear, listen to bad music on the internet, or watch scary movies. We have parental locks on all of our devices at our house but believe it or not some kids do not have locks at all. Certain words at our house are not allowed and are considered swear words. "STUPID" and "HATE" are two of the words not allowed.

It is really hard to get those words out of your child's mouths, especially after they have heard them at other people's houses. They play with their friends who are allowed to talk that way or listen to bad music and think when they come home, they are allowed to also. After all, it is fun to be bad; it's just not fun to get disciplined for it. Right?

We definitely try to protect our children as all parents do. We probably over protect them in some people's opinion. Sure, we like to keep them in our own little "bubble" we can say. As much as we would all love to be able to protect our children from everything we think is bad, let me remind you it is impossible. These are just some examples. There are so many more.

I am the parent who always has to be the one to come let the other parents know when I've seen a behavior I've never witnessed before from my kids. I can definitely see why other parents get offended about it, because it might seem as if I am pointing out their kid's behavior as an intolerable behavior to me. I get it No parent wants to have the bad kid. Some parents might think I am over reacting. You are raising your children and you know what goes on in your home. You are fully aware of the behaviors and language you allow.

Here is where reality finally kicks in. When the tables are turned! When you get the teacher notes from school and when you start seeing your kids push their limits. This is when you start to think, "Am I a bad parent? Is my kid the bad kid? Where did he hear these things from? Who taught him that? Is he hanging out with the wrong kids. Are they are too old for him? Is this just a stage all boys go through?" The questions can go on forever.

Truth is, all of it, some of it, or none of it could be true at all. You are not a bad parent. Your kid is not a bad kid. His behavior is bad. Hey, I get it. I know I have seen some kids who are bad every time I see them and every parent who has ever met them only has bad stories to tell about the kid. That is a bad kid I agree. I don't blame it entirely on the kid though I believe if the kid is out of control it is probably because there has not been enough discipline and now it is starting to be too late. He might be spending too much time with older kids where certain behaviors are expected and considered normal. If they are hanging out with the wrong crowd, they are the wrong crowd. Remember, being bad is fun, because it is not allowed at home. If they can get away with it somewhere else why would it be any different at home? The problem with younger kids spending time with older kids is older kids know how to stick together. Older kids can talk younger kids into doing things they normally would not or even think about.

Your kid might not have heard the new words they bring home from you. They might not have learned the new behaviors you have seen from you either. Just because they did not get it from you does not mean they are not guilty of doing something. So yes, your kid is perfect around you. Maybe they are coming home and telling on their friends because they are guilty too and do not want to be disciplined. Maybe they are innocent and the older kids are trying to see them get in trouble. We might never know the true story. Just because he didn't get it from you does not mean he did not have fun with his new words and behaviors too. Us parents know who is most likely telling the truth and who is telling a lie. Do not lie to yourself. "**<u>NOT MY KID!</u>**" Guess what... it probably was your kid. This is something that took me a long time to believe myself. So, when they come to tell you, "guess what so and so did?" Remember to ask them, "What did you do?"

Chapter 4
He Started It!

The Mama and I are pretty particular about who babysits our children. We have always been paranoid about it. It just always made us nervous to leave the boys with someone new. Still to this day, we only let them stay with family. I admit, it is a bit easier to consider a new sitter now, when it comes to Camden and Conner because they are older. I guess our attitude about it started to change once they could talk. We are the same way with Cohen as we were with the oldest two, when it comes to being nervous. I don't think the paranoia is quite as bad though because his big brothers would be with him. It's easy for me to say there is less paranoia, but we still are not going to leave Cohen with a different sitter other than family.

Sitters can be an iffy subject when it comes to our boys, mostly because they are our whole world. Leaving them with anyone other than family just seems crazy, especially when they are babies. It's super hard to trust someone new sometimes with something so precious.

Sitters are one thing, but what about when they visit a friend's house? We used to worry about the parents being

mean or not keeping an eye on them. Sure, if they are playing with their friends at our house, we don't feel like we are babysitting. We don't want other parents to feel that way either. Sometimes, however, it does seem as if we are sitters for their friends because there is usually always someone over. It's usually no big deal because their friends are pretty good. We wouldn't want another parent to feel like they are babysitting, but I would hope they would at least, pay attention to what they are doing. After all, they are boys. Boys seem to find themselves in some curious situations at times. Curious for them making new discoveries and curious for us trying to figure out what they were doing.

By the time we finally let them play at their friend's houses without us, we were starting to get a little more comfortable with them being away. Away with someone, other than the regular sitters, that is.

So, we are finally comfortable they will be safe under someone else's supervision, but here comes a new issue: How will they behave? We know our guys are good kids and very respectful, but will they do something another parent won't like?

Even if I am not a huge fan of the other parents, I still want my kids to behave. I know, when a few boys get together, it can become a bit rowdy at times, after all, I was a boy once too. The Mama and I are pretty lenient when it comes to crazy kids. We do have a house full of boys. You could probably guess, we are used to a lot more "crazy" than someone with only one or two. I just wonder, do the other parents know what they are getting into with two boys plus their own? We are pretty lucky the boy's neighborhood friends have good parents. Most of our houses have large trampolines in the backyard, so a royal rumble is never uncommon.

There are a few instances that stand out to me with one of their friends down the road. The boy is a pretty good boy most of the time, however, he is also sneaky. Then again, what eight-year-old boy does that not describe? I remember walking the kids half way to his house. Conner and him met up, and I watched the boy push Conner in the grass. I yelled to him, "do you want me to tell your mom?" Remember, I do have three boys, I definitely would not tell his mom. If anyone is used to horseplay, it's us. I guess it was my "mama bird mode," coming out.

There is one more time which stands out to me. Actually, it's the same situation, but happens multiple times. The boys would ask to go to his house almost every day in the summer. They would be over there all day probably, if I did not make them come home to check in every 30 minutes. The boy's mother would set a clock for them so they were not late. Sometimes they would all play so good together. Other times, one would come home mad or crying. I heard only their side of the story, so maybe I am also still in the "not my kid" stage too.

The boys would tell us what they were doing and for some reason out of nowhere the other boy would beat them up or throw something at one of them. Conner was a lot smaller. Even though he would come home he was never the one crying. He was usually just mad. Camden is bigger than Conner, but smaller than the other boy. Camden was usually the one crying. Sometimes we could not tell if he was hurt physically or if it was just his feelings. When it comes to Conner, he was used to being picked on by his big brother, so he was usually just mad.

For some reason their stories were always: "He started it!" Sound familiar? From the behaviors I have witnessed from this boy, I can't say it was very hard to believe. On occasion the arguments or fights would be worse than normal and my boys would be sent home. Later that day, or the following day, they would all be playing again. Sometimes they would get along, other times, not so much. Eventually we discovered Conner got along much better alone with the boy than Camden did. Camden would not always want to go to his house. Conner liked to play with him, probably because Conner would play whatever the boy wanted. Camden does not like to be bossed around by other kids, still to this day. Conner does not like getting bossed around either, but he is way more laid back, when it comes down to it.

This boy definitely had his mother fooled, I think. She was definitely in the "not my kid stage." I've been there too and sometimes, still am. Or, maybe she just knows kids eventually need a break from each other after a while. She is a pretty nice lady, so I'd assume if she knew both sides of the story, she would let us know. Maybe, maybe not. Especially if she heard the side we did and her kid was to blame. Either way, she took care of it her way and I'm ok with it.

For some reason, they all stopped playing together one day. We don't hear them ask to go to his house anymore either. I never asked why. I guess, I can just assume it is safe to say, maybe it was true all along. Maybe, just maybe: **HE STARTED IT!**

Chapter 5
Store Tantrums

Chapter 5
Store Tantrums

It's about 1 p.m. Saturday afternoon and you just walk into your favorite grocery store. By favorite I am clearly being sarcastic. You haven't been shopping in probably 2 weeks and your cabinets and refrigerator are completely empty, so you know you will be here for a while. The place is packed and you are starting to second guess your decision about going shopping at this exact time and day. You are already here so you decide let's do this.

You start in the front of the store because that is where you came in at. You have to even wait in line just to pick out green peppers. Some people are in a hurry and some have nothing better to do but take their time. You see a woman with 2 kids in a cart and they are just not loving the shopping experience either. They are throwing a fit. They are mad and crying. The mother is embarrassed and just completely stressed out. She only has her cart half full and still has to wait in the super long Saturday afternoon checkout lanes.

This sounds like the beginning to a horror story I know. Trust me I've been there. I have been in both situations: the mother's with the two angry kids, and the lonely guy getting his long overdue shopping trip done. Let me tell you I would much rather be the lonely guy shopping.

I have been in the mom's shoes more than once and with 3 kids not just 2. It really is so easy to get very overwhelmed by the tantrums and the rude people who also do not want to experience your kids' tantrums. It is hard to deal with it the first couple of times you have to deal with it, but hate it or not you will either get used to it or learn to ignore it. Yup I said it, "... the first couple of times." Truth is it happens and it happens to all of us. Even the best parents in the world with the most well-behaved children have dealt with this. It's very easy to spot the people without kids because they are the only people in the entire store getting irritated by it. You can also tell the new parents because they are the ones getting stressed out and embarrassed. It is easy to get frustrated and angry about it but that will not make the kids any happier.

The kids do not want to be at the store any more than you do. They could be hungry, tired, or maybe they missed a nap. Maybe they wanted a certain toy and they are not allowed to have it. I learned sometimes you have to give in. It is so easy to give your kid the toy they wanted at the beginning of the trip or better yet make them hold out until you are half way done. They will want to earn the toy so they will be pretty good until they see it. When you see they are about to start acting up get the toy and let them play until you are done. Even if you do not want to buy it you can use our excuse and tell them the cashier must have forgotten to put it in the bag. Sure, the kids will be upset in the car but it will have saved you and other people in the store the tantrum experience. Of course, this might not always work and there might be other options but this always worked for us.

So many people will say things such as, "Don't give in to them, you are spoiling them." Or my favorite, "My kid wouldn't do that!" My argument to that is, they are completely wrong. They are not spoiled they are appeased for the moment and it most absolutely will be their kid one day if it has not been already. You are definitely not a bad parent for trying to keep your kid calm. There will be more times than not that your kids will be good. Chances are, even if you cannot stop the tantrums most likely you will not see any of the people in the store again anyway. The best thing to do is just get done what you need to get done. This is the best time for you, otherwise you would be at home I'm sure. Kids will be hungry, kids will be tired, and kids will be bored. If you have more than one, they will definitely fight.

I have been lucky enough to go shopping without kids or alone with just one of them and it definitely is a lot easier. Most of the time The Mama and I will go while either the oldest two are at school or one will stay home or in the car while the other goes shopping. If I'm alone and see another parent with kids shopping and I see the insanity they are dealing with, I can just smile and pray for them to have patience. With kids we definitely all need lots of patience. Always, if I am in line and a parent with kids end up directly behind me, I let them go in front of me, because I have been there more times than one. It definitely does get easier as the kids get older. I am confident all parents can relate. Always try to keep your cool. You definitely do not want anyone witnessing, "your" **STORE TANTRUM!**

CHAPTER 6
How Do You Do It?

Life as a parent is busy. If you have one kid or three no matter what, its busy. Life is busy before we have kids with juggling a full-time job, a mortgage, bills, home repairs, and whatever else life throws at us at the time. So, we already have all these responsibilities and we want to throw kids into the mix? What are we crazy? If we aren't yet we will be within about five years! With all joking aside reality is kids are great. They really are the best part of life.

When people would ask The Mama and I when we were planning on having kids, we would usually have the same answer. We would say we wanted to be financially stable first. My Uncle replied to my answer one time that stuck with me to this day. He said, "If you are going to wait until you are financially stable you will never have kids." To some people this might have seemed kind of negative, but let me be clear, my uncle is not a negative person. He is full of knowledge and highly respected throughout my entire family. His advice was probably an unwritten factor in part of our decision when we decided we were ready to start having children. That little piece of advice had so much truth to it I have even found myself giving it to other people thinking of starting a family.

Sure, it sounds great to have all your ducks in a row. Go to school, get a good job, get a nice home, get married, then start a family. Typical American dream, right? Well, maybe not for everyone, but it was for us. The Mama was still continuing school finishing her Bachelor's degree after we had Camden. Conner came along 16 months later. We definitely thought we were ready for kids but I think sometimes the truth is you can never really be ready, at least until your third one that is.

I have been put in so many stressful situations with these boys and it seemed as if the day was never going to end, from tantrums due to teething to growing pains. Let me tell you it can be so hard at times. For the most part these are the things people do not see.

There are other times when you are out in public with friends or family, or even just as a family with or without The Mama, and the boys are super good. I remember a time before Cohen was born, I took Camden and Conner to a new Mexican restaurant. The restaurant had been around for many years, but we had never been there. I just happen to have been having a lucky day I guess. These guys were both getting along and behaving as good little boys should. The waitress, cook, and even the owner all came over to the table to compliment me on such a great job parenting. Times like these really make a parent feel good. I was really proud of my guys that day.

Then there are the "OTHER DAYS." These are the days every parent knows of way too well. The days when the kids don't want to listen, don't want to behave, cannot get along, or throw tantrums no matter where you are and they do not care who is around. These are the embarrassing days for us parents when people without kids, or people who forgot what it was like to have small kids, stare at us in the stores or give us the dirty looks. We know what they are thinking, we know they are just as annoyed with it as we are, but it all comes with the package.

The Mama and I work opposite schedules so there are many times each of us have all the boys while the other is at work or sleeping. I remember another occasion when Camden and Conner were a couple of years younger and we were at a different restaurant. The waiter came over and started talking to me about how great he thought it was that I took my boys to lunch just the three of us. While talking to him I was giving him our order and Conner tried sliding out from under the table. Without missing a beat, I put my leg up to block him and continued to order. The waiter just started laughing and said, "Wow, you are really good that!" I just smiled, put Conner back in his seat, and said, "It's just a parent thing I guess." Our waiter I am assuming did not have any kids, because I did not really see what was so spectacular about what just happened. Though, the compliment was appreciated.

There are other times you will be at home and there is so much to do. Anyone who has a home knows there is always something to be done from cooking, dishes, and the dreaded laundry, to in home repairs. Juggling all this with three kids can be challenging at times especially when they are really small. Now that they are getting a bit older, they are quite helpful with chores such as taking care of the dog, cleaning up, and putting their folded clothes away. We like to do as many of the home repair projects as we can during the day while they are in school so it does not take our time away from them though sometimes certain projects cannot wait. For these projects usually we try to find something for them to do, let them just play, or she will take them somewhere fun. If those are not options, we just take breaks throughout the project to play with them.

Some people get stressed about certain things a lot. Everything has to be done right now as quick as possible with no interruptions. Here is the news flash, rather you have kids or not, life happens. Not every day is going to be easy. We will learn from all of them. So, you ask, **<u>"HOW DO YOU DO IT?"</u>** My answer is no one knows how we do it. We are parents and it just gets done, because it has to.

Chapter 7
It's Time To Go Home

It's so nice sometimes to finally be able to set the worries of life aside for a few hours. It's nice to take time and go to dinner with the family or your friends and laugh and have fun. Sometimes it's nice to just be able to go outside to sit, relax, and not have to do yard work. It's so nice to be able to get lost in a totally different reality other than the normal day to day rush we are so used to living. As adults, moments like these are moments we all look forward to. As a parent, moments like these are moments we cherish. Sometimes we wish certain moments like these would last forever.

Kids are similar to adults in this situation because they too are also used to the same things. They live in the same home every day. They have their same bedroom with the same toys. Sometimes it is super fun when they find an old toy they had forgotten about or find a new use for something old. It's still all the same day to day routine with an occasional trip to the grocery store or somewhere boring they really do not want to be. Sometimes they get to go to the park!

Going to the park, to another friend's house, or even for a bike ride and picnic most likely seem to them the same as going to dinner with friends and family or how sitting and enjoying our fresh cut lawn feels to us. Just as we get wrapped up in our moments and do not want them to end so do they. In most cases going to the park every day and picnics are not an everyday occurrence for us. These moments are all definitely a great time for us to sit back and unwind. The difference between us and a toddler is we know these moments have to eventually end. Kids have so much fun during these times always and it often becomes extremely hard to bring them back to "their reality" when it is time to pack up.

Now that Camden and Conner are getting older it is way easier to get them to be ready when we are. They are great with telling time and before we even get to where we are going, we are always sure to let them know how much time they have and what time we will be leaving. There are some occasions, when the boundaries are pushed, mostly when it comes to going swimming. Since we know that leaving might be an issue at the pool, we start telling them about 5 minutes before we are really ready to go that it is time. They do not have tantrums, but we hear, "I just want to go under one more time," about 10 times. It definitely seems to get easier as they get a bit older and can learn to be aware of time.

How about before they could tell time? Now that was a whole other issue. I think it is fair to say, all of us parents have to deal with our kids throwing a fit even if it is as small as just some alligator tears when it's time to be on our way. Let's face it they already live in a totally different mindset than we do. Then we add something new and out of the ordinary for them to do that they love, and just makes them lose all sense of awareness around them. Something to make them completely focus on this new fun. Now it's time for us to make it stop all of sudden. This has to be devastating especially if they have not completely worn themselves out yet. Talk about throwing a wrench in the gears. Their world is so much more fun than ours. Everything is so much more intense. Everything is bigger. Everything is exciting. Why would they want to snap out of that zone they are in and go back to their normal reality. Especially, when you just made their already amazing life that much more amazing?

The answer is: they don't want to. They don't want to get out of the new reality you have just taken them to. They are not able to understand yet that it eventually has to end. We struggled with this issue for a few years with both our oldest boys so far and I'm sure Cohen will have his turn.

When they are two and three years old, kids are just learning their letters and numbers. How could we get them to understand time especially, when they still can't even count to 30 yet?

One day it just happened without out even planning it. I had to make a trip to the hardware store and The Mama was sleeping because she had to work later that night. Camden, Conner, and I got in the car and drove to the hardware store to pick up what we needed. While we were there, we ate hotdogs on the way out as we always do and drove a bit of a scenic route home.

Our little adventure took us almost exactly one hour. This was it! This was my " AH-HA MOMENT!" After we pulled into the driveway before I unbuckled the boys, I asked them if they had fun. I then told them we were gone for an hour. They are still little and still have no idea about time so why did I even tell them?

The next few short trips we would take I would make sure to tell them if it was going to be about an hour. Next, I would say, "Do you remember how long it took to go to the hardware store and back?" They always said yes, even if they really did forget. I'll never know. I would then tell them, "It's going to take about that long." I did this for a long while until they could tell time. When I knew we would be gone for two or three hours I'd say, "It's as long as going to the hardware store and back, and then going to the hardware store and back one more time. So, we have to do it two times."

When we would go to the park or go somewhere fun and I planned on being gone only an hour or so, I'd always use this. They were still unable to tell time by looking at the numbers on the clock, but by now they were able to have an awareness of it. The crying still came sometimes and I'd have to remind them they were told how long they would be allowed to play. Of course, it did not always work, but I would definitely call this a success. A huge Dad win!

When the kids start throwing their fits and having tantrums it is so easy to get lost in the moment and get upset too. I have been angry. I have yelled. You name it. We are all guilty of losing our cool sometimes. I have caught myself losing mine. It doesn't help things at all. It only makes matters worse, because now the kids are screaming for a totally different reason. Let me tell you; it only takes one time for you to realize you look like a jerk and just embarrassed yourself to snap back to reality. You look way better as a parent and a person when you can keep your cool with and angry toddler no matter what sort of problems might be going on. If you are not bothered at all by the tantrums, the kids will notice and I assure the tantrums will not last long.

So, the next time you are planning to do something fun, new, and exciting outside of your toddler's reality. Remember what could potentially happen when it's time for it to end. Be prepared for the meltdown. Make sure that you too, are ready for when, **<u>ITS TIME TO GO HOME!</u>"**

Chapter 8
We Are Not On The Same Schedule

It's 7:00 a.m. the alarm clock is ringing. Time to wake the boys up to help them start getting ready for school. Usually I lay in bed and hit the snooze button a few times or wait until the second alarm begins to go off around 7:30 a.m. Most of the time at least one of the boys are already awake. Now it is 7:30 a.m. and I have to get out of bed. If Camden and Conner are still asleep it's time to wake them up. School starts at 8:48 a.m. no matter if we are on time or not.

Now that they are getting older most days are fairly easy to get them going in the morning. Most of the time at least one of them is already awake playing video games or playing in the basement in the toy room. Just because they are awake doesn't mean they are ready for school though. Either The Mama or myself needs to tell them to get dressed, remind them to brush their teeth, and have some yogurt or cereal for breakfast.

The Mama is pretty good about making sure the boys have their clothes set out for school for the next day. She almost always already has their lunches packed the night before too. There are some rare occasions things are not set out and lunches need to be packed, but hardly ever. I think she knows it would probably be chaos in our house in the morning if it were not already taken care of the night before, especially if she is at work.

It really is nice now that the boys are old enough to pick out their own clothes and get dressed themselves. We really save a lot of time with them being able to handle those things. Camden makes his own cereal in the morning and will sometimes help out Conner. Conner is able to on his own, but if the milk is full... the bowl usually over flows. Most of the time they just eat yogurt for breakfast, its fast, easy, and they love it. It's not bad for them either, so what not to like? Now Conner can even tie his shoes. After they both brush their teeth, they are ready to go. I really love this part of these guys getting older they really do seem so big and grown up at times. The two oldest are pretty self-sufficient when it comes to getting ready in the morning.

Then there is Cohen. Cohen is still a baby so, of course, we wonder, "Where is he while all of this is going on?" Well... after the kids are awake for the day and they are getting motivated to start getting ready it's time to get the baby. He is usually awake by now with all the commotion happening around his bedroom in the morning. Unless, he was awake prior to all of it. Time to change him and get his bottle ready. Most of the time either The Mama or myself is feeding him while the other keeps the oldest two on track. Cohen is pretty easy unless his diaper leaks and he needs a bath first thing in the morning. Even then he is so small it doesn't take very long. The hardest part about Cohen is waiting for him to finish his bottle. Sometimes it takes a really long time. More good news for our family though is soon he will be able to hold his own bottle and The Mama and I can focus on other morning task until he is done. After he is fed and changed again, we change his clothes and we are out the door, off to school we go.

This does all seem like a lot is happening in the morning and if the baby is mad and crying for some reason we have not figured out quite yet, it can seem extremely hectic from the outside looking in. I can assure you at times it is chaos, but it is a controlled chaos usually. If it were not for The Mama making sure so many morning tasks were prepped it could be a disaster sometimes. I know this because, it has been before.

Things do seem so much easier today than they did about three or four years ago. The two oldest boys are sixteen months apart so there have been many times we felt as if we had twins. Often when we went to the grocery store or out to dinner people would ask if they were. They were both in diapers at the same time. They loved the same toys so there was two of everything. We needed the double stroller which was way too wide to really take anywhere unless we were outside. We did save a lot of money with them being so close in age, because we had a lot of hand me down clothes for Conner.

When they were toddlers getting them to do things was not always easy. The Mama and I would usually wake up at least two hours early for everything. After all, we had twice the diapers to change, twice the breakfast to prepare and feed them, and twice the amount of time helping them to get dressed. When we wanted them to wake up and start getting ready for the day it usually consisted with a ton of distractions. They are boys after all, so if they were not staring at the television, they were either making a lot of "VROOM VROOM" noises, or the living room would be a royal rumble.

Sometimes getting them dressed was even a chore for us in the morning. Mostly for me I'd say. These guys were so close to the same size, I would sometimes put Camden's shirts on Conner and wow would that seem like a catastrophe to Camden. I know what you are thinking... "Why wouldn't I have their clothes in separate dressers?" We did have separate dressers so if the clothes were mixed it was most likely me who put them away any way. The Mama always knew whose was whose. Now that they are older, I usually lay all their clothes straight and have them put everything away themselves.

When they were old enough, we would tell them to get dressed after we picked out their clothes. We would give them a few minutes to do it and sometimes walk back in the bedroom to see them playing. We had Velcro shoes for them as well. We would tell them right before we were ready to leave, "Go get your shoes on guys." Since they were Velcro and so easy to put on, I always thought this was a pretty simple task. We would sometimes be ready to walk out of the door and still no shoes. Sometimes, and still to this day I cannot explain it, one shoe comes up missing. Some days we could not find them at all. For the first 4 years of having those guys I don't think we were on time for anything besides work.

How could we make things smoother? Well, we figured out the obvious first. Take their shoes off in the same place every day. That sounds obvious sure, but with a toddler it seems impossible. Even when we take them off at the front door there are still times, they sneak them for some reason or another to play. Sometimes, I swore they hid them on purpose to make me crazy. No shirt, no shoes, no service does not apply to a toddler if you are carrying them. I can't even begin to count how many times in the spring and summer we would carry the boys to the car and right to a basket because of missing shoes.

The best and easiest way we learned to get these guys to get ready quickly for us was to make it game. They are after all brothers, are they not? It's just natural I guess for brothers to be competitive. I say I guess, because I only had sisters so it is only a guess from what we have experienced. We would make it a race. A race to see who could get dressed faster. A race to see who could get their shoes on faster. A race to see who could get to the car faster and get buckled in fastest. We still race to the car all the time. The Dada usually always loses, no biggy I'm slow anyway. We have so many races so often, no one remembers who wins most we just try to win at the moment. There are other ways to get the little ones moving faster I know, but this has worked for us extremely well.

Yelling and getting stressed out definitely is not the answer. It only makes things worse. Kids do not seem to work very well under pressure. Kids are wired differently than adults. They are wired for having fun, eating, and sleeping. What we have to do as adults is not important to them yet. There is no way they could even understand, our schedule or responsibilities. Their schedule is having fun. Make it fun and it will work a whole lot easier. Remember, **WE ARE NOT ON THE SAME SCHEDULE!**

Chapter 9
There Is Always Nap Time!

The kids are acting up again! Sometimes I swear it's like I'm talking to myself. Maybe I'm talking to the walls. Who knows, maybe it is just my imagination. Whatever it is, for some reason sometimes these kids just will not seem to listen. They just do whatever they want and no matter what The Dada says... oh well. Right?

We can talk about all kinds of times these guys wouldn't listen. Sometimes their fighting I think blocks their ear drums to where they cannot hear me. All they can focus on is why the other one made them so angry. The smallest things can cause an argument sometimes. No matter if it's because one of them is wearing a shirt that does not belong to them or one of them is singing the wrong words to a song.

Sometimes I feel like we have tried everything. We have done time outs, separating them, lots of yelling, and even though I don't like to admit it, even spankings. Time outs work sometimes. We use the one minute for each year the child is old rule. This does ok for when it is a punishment for just one kid, but when it's both that need it, we usually stick with Conner's age. If they are really bad the time out is ten minutes. Usually the longer time out works pretty well because they get bored and often fall asleep. Separating them works out ok too. We live in a small house and they share a bedroom so separating them is not always easy. We try our best to keep yelling at a minimum, because we know it only shows we are annoyed and usually does not help. Spankings worked ok for me when I was little. I guess associating pain with bad behavior is a good way to deter it, however I think I can maybe count on both hands how many spankings we have given. I don't like the idea of hurting my children. Some people might argue there is a difference between spankings and abuse. I believe there is a pretty fine line. A quick 1-time reminder spanking is a lot different than a 20-time butt whoopin. It's been said, "This hurts me than it hurts you," so why do it if it hurts yourself? In our case spankings have proved to be pretty ineffective. There are other ways we have tried too.

We tried taking things away, groundings, we even tried canceling RSVPs for birthday parties. Taking things away works pretty well especially when it is something they really enjoy. Grounding works great as long as you can stick to the time frame. Threatening to cancel their RSVP to birthday parties has proven to be quite effective. The problem with canceling an RSVP though is the parents of the other kid already paid for your kid to be there. So as a result of canceling for our kid it also cost someone else money. Unless your kid is super bad or if you are going to just drop off the gift I wouldn't recommend actually canceling. Thankfully the THREAT of canceling works very well.

We thought we had another good idea. We would threaten to call the police. It worked for a little while, but in our case, we know so many police officers calling the police was more of a reward. Uncle Josh works for the State Police. If a stranger would get in trouble by him, I'm sure he would be pretty scary. That's not the case for the boys though. They always have so much fun with Uncle Josh so calling the police is a good thing for them. The same goes for the other people we know in law enforcement. They are always so good to the kids a threat to call them for bad behavior is really a worthless threat. I have been told threatening calling the police is a bad thing, because I would be making my children afraid of someone who is out in the world trying to protect them. I see that point and 100% agree with it. I admit looking back at that threat it was not a very good idea at all.

If none of these ideas will work, what will? JAIL! Threatening jail works really well. My kids are not afraid of police, but they are scared to death of jail, prison, and juvie. We used to tell them they would go to baby jail and there are only mean kids in baby jail. The idea was a pretty good idea too, until they finally figured out they would get an honest answer from their Uncle if they asked if there was such thing as baby jail. Thanks Uncle Josh.

We found videos of some pretty mean looking people online getting arrested and crying because they were scared to go to jail. It really did work and still does. Even though it is a controversial topic amongst some of my family and friends. I am totally fine with my kids being fearful of jail. I'd be scared of jail. I'm not sure why anyone wouldn't be.

I definitely believe that any of these are worth trying except threatening police especially if your child does not have a close relationship with any. Different situations require different punishments some harsher than others. Sometimes some work well sometimes we have to try more than one multiple times. My boys are for the most part almost always pretty good boys. They listen usually and do their chores. They are great in school and pretty respectful. They are still kids though. I get it "boys will be boys." One of the most important pieces of advice I have been given is, "YOU HAVE TO STAY CONSISTENT." There is one thing to always remember also is if nothing else works and you are on your last straw. The one thing that has never failed us. **THERE IS ALWAYS NAP TIME!**

CHAPTER 10
Jacob's Wallet

Throughout life there are so many things we learn that make us who we are. We are brought up to do things certain ways. We are taught what things are good and bad. We learn what to like and dislike. There are many behaviors we learn by being told. Other behaviors are learned by what we witness. Not everything can be taught in a book. Honesty and integrity are two of them.

We raise our kids to be good boys. We teach them to be good to others and animals and be respectful. We want them to grow up to be good men. Sometimes when we take a look around us and see how scary the world can be, we wonder, "How can we shield them from all of this negativity? How can we protect them from all of this hate and violence? How can we keep them in a safe zone or giant bubble?" Next, we realize... we can't. We can't make them blind to the violence, the hate, the crime, and all the negativity that is everywhere in this world. All we can do is protect them. All we can do is guide them. How can we do it? We can do it by leading by example...

It was sometime in July. A typical hot, sunny, summer day. Camden, Conner, and I had some errands to run. Cam was probably no older than 4 years old. I remember carrying Conner most of the time that day. We had to go to the grocery store and I needed to go to the phone store while we were out. I knew the phone store is usually pretty busy so I decided I'd try to go there before we went to get lunch. On the way we listened to music, talked about what we had to do, and what we wanted to eat for lunch. The phone store is in a strip mall at a pretty busy intersection a couple cities over from ours. The parking lot is really small for the amount of traffic that comes in and out of there. We were pretty lucky we found a front row parking spot. It was probably meant to be.

Of course, no one would have known what was going to happen that day. After I parked, I got out of the car and unbuckled Camden on his side. I always shut the door after to make sure he did not run out before I unbuckled Conner on the other side. I went over to Conner's side unbuckled him and had Camden climb over to the side we were at so we could go into the store.

We did get a front row parking spot but we were still about four stores from the phone store. As we were walking, I was holding both the boy's hands. Of course, I am way taller than the two of them so I'm always looking down. We get about half way to the phone store and there it was... It was right there in between two parked cars with no one around. A brown wallet.

As soon as I saw it I took the boys over to it and picked it up. Camden, I remember was pretty excited. It was almost as if we had stumbled upon a pirate's secret long lost treasure. I knew we did not have a lot of time before whose ever wallet this was would be gone not realizing they had lost it until it was too late. So, we walked in the store the car was parked closest to and asked the cashier if anyone had asked about a lost wallet. I asked her to look with me as I opened it to see if there was a license inside. The license inside said it belonged to a man named Jacob. We walked around the small store asking everyone if they were missing a wallet. Jacob was not there. We left and continued to go in every store in the strip mall. Still no Jacob. I told the boys after the phone store we were going to make a special trip to the police station to turn it in.

When we came to the phone store we asked around in there as well and looked for anyone who might match the picture. Still no luck. It was our turn in line I was purchasing a speaker that would work with my phone. After the cashier rang me up Camden asked, "Are we gonna use Jacob's money?" I quickly explained to him how using Jacob's money would be wrong, would not be nice, and since it was not our money, it would be stealing. I made sure to give the cashier my license while I gave him my debit card just in case, he questioned it too. He and I must have both been thinking the same thing because he chuckled and thanked me while waving my license in the air gently.

We finished up and took our bags. We were on our way out when a woman stopped me and said, "It's really nice that you are teaching your boys to do the right thing." Without missing a beat, I replied "I'm not teaching boys. I'm training men." We both smiled as we walked out of the store. I couldn't believe I just said that, it was perfect.

As we were walking out of the store we were still talking about Jacob and how he is going to be sad when he discovers he is missing his wallet. Right before we get to our car I happen to look over as a car was driving by, somehow through the tinted windows I could see inside. There he was in the passenger side of a small SUV. That was Jacob! "HEY! HEY!," I yelled. I had to be as loud as I could. I couldn't believe he heard me. The car stopped and I held his wallet in the air. He got out and we could see it was definitely him! There he was, it was Jacob! I gave him his wallet, he then opened it up and smiled really big. Afterward, he shook my hand and thanked us.

Jacob got back in the car and drove away. I put the boys in their seats and our bags in the car then we headed to lunch. All the way to lunch Camden was talking about that wallet. The whole time at lunch too. He talked about that wallet and what we did for a really long time after that. I think him seeing the way Jacob was so happy really had an effect on him from that day. I know Camden still remembers Jacob's last name even.

Moments like these do not come up very often. I'm sure there will be plenty more as life goes on. Maybe not finding wallets, but life is full of lessons and opportunities. Jacob's wallet had cash and a few checks in it. There was an opportunity to do two things that day. What was right or what was wrong. Thankfully for Jacob, I was raised to do what was right, and the wrong never even crossed my mind. I am not sure how much money was in that wallet, but I assure you the memories and life lessons I shared with my boys that day were worth way more money than could ever even fit in **JACOB'S WALLET.**

CHAPTER 11
The Cool Kid

True friends are hard to come by sometimes. Some people are not lucky enough to have any. Fortunately, I have been blessed with many. We all have many kinds of friends. There is the one buddy who will bring you a can of gas twenty miles away in the middle of the night. There is the buddy who will buy you a pop every time he sees you when you go out. Then there is the buddy you used to know but still keep on social media. There probably are a lot more to list.

How about the one buddy who will walk by your side through a tornado. The one guy who will trust you with his life. The one guy who gets super excited every time he sees you. The guy who will always tell you the truth not even caring if it hurts because he is so honest and it's not even a second thought. The one buddy who is as sad and happy as you are on your worst and best days.

I have some of those buddies. I have three for sure. They are my boys, Camden, Conner, and Cohen. I know I have said before and heard it plenty of times before too, "I'm their dad not their friend." I can agree with that SOMETIMES. I know I can't always be their friend. Sure, there is a time for discipline. There is a time for fun too. I like to think I am a good father. I have been doing ok with it for the last 7 years or so.

When I hear people tell me, "You can't be their friend!" I have to mostly disagree. Although I can understand their point. I feel I can be their friend just not always. There is a time the two have to be separate. I believe I can be their friend and a good father at the same time. When I was growing up my dad was one of my best friends and definitely one of those guys I was describing while describing my boys in the beginning. We used to always go fishing, go on bike rides, play catch, and spend a lot of time in the garage where I learned something new almost every day. I cannot remember my parents ever really yelling at me or my sisters. There were a few times that stand out to me, but not many.

I think being your child's friend is a good thing. I never wanted to let my parents down. I valued our relationship too much. So, I guess what it comes down to is... how early is too early? Is there a certain age which is best to try and be their friend or does it just depend on the moment? I'm leaning more toward going with the moment.

I try to do some of the same things with my boys as my dad did with me. Part of the reason is it's what I know. The other part is it's what I like. There are so many memories I have that always stuck with me. I try to pass these memories down to my guys by letting them experience some of the same things I did growing up.

When they are toddlers, they are so much fun. They always want to be with Daddy. They always want to play and have fun. We are their best friends. We are all they know when they are that small. We play what they want to play. Do all the things they want to do and follow all of their own rules to games. No wonder they sometimes look at us as friends. They don't know the difference yet. Every day is always so much fun, there is always something new and exciting to do. Playing catch, playing with blocks and cars, and running around at the park.

Eventually they get a little bit older and start to make new friends. There are kids next door and down the street. When they start to notice them, we think, "What a great thing it would be to introduce them." They start to play with each other and have a lot of fun. It is definitely a good thing to start introducing your children to other kids early. Introducing them early in life helps with different social skills. One of the most important in my opinion is sharing. Trust me if they can learn to share it will save gallons of tears.

There are so many great reasons to help find them friends. Another reason besides it giving you a little break from rebuilding the Lego house you just rebuilt for the sixth time. It also gives you a minute to catch your breath and let your arms relax from playing airplane all day too. There is one reason however, that is not so good...

After the last two or three years of playing with the same little guy and you making a new best friend yourself; now you just gave him to someone else to enjoy. Remember the sentence a couple paragraphs back when I talked about sharing. Well maybe sometimes it's not so easy after all. My guys are seriously some of the coolest people I know. They like almost all of the same things I do. We always get along. We are almost equal at sports for the moment anyway. They always want to have fun. Kids are usually honest. What's not to like? That describes the perfect best friend to me.

One summer day Camden and I woke up early together. We stayed really quiet to make sure we did not wake up Conner or The Mama. We drove to pick up breakfast for everyone and coffee for The Mama to surprise them. When we arrived back home everyone was awake and excited to eat. Afterward, the boys and I went outside to play some catch. We made up some new games and were having such a great time. We played until about noon. Around this time one of the neighbor boys woke up and started riding his bike. My guys noticed him and immediately stopped playing with me and asked if they could ride their bikes with him. Of course, I told them to go ahead. For the first time since I was probably their age, I had the feeling I was feeling at that moment. I was usually the last to get picked for teams in school. I've said it before, sports were never really my thing. For my boys' team I was always first pick. I was always the coolest person. Finally, I was, "THE COOL KID." Well, at least until the new kid. I will admit I was pretty sad. As they started to run for their bikes, they both stopped and looked at me as if they felt a little guilty for leaving me to clean up and stop playing so they could play with someone else. I am pretty sure that is the part that got me most.

There was one more time I can remember I had the same feeling. Santa brought the boys rockets for Christmas. Not just the little plastic rockets you find laying in the toy box. The real rockets. The models we have to build and are able to launch a thousand feet in the air. Each of the boys had one. When we finally had an opportunity to build them it was really cold outside. Conner did not have too long of patience with his so I ended up finishing his until it was time to put on the stickers. After the rockets were built, we could not wait until the next day when the glue would finally be dry.

The next day we woke up and had breakfast. The boys played some video games with The Mama for a bit in the morning until they remembered today was the day. The day of our rocket launch. They were disappointed to find out we could not launch them because it was way too windy outside. They decided they would finish getting ready for the day and head to a neighbor's house to play for awhile. After the baby was finally asleep for his nap, I noticed the wind had died down quite a bit outside, so I decided to pack up the car with the rockets and go pick up the boys while The Mama stayed with the baby.

I drove to the neighbor's house where I seen my guys along with about four other boys playing what looked like a game of tag. I just stopped the car in front of the house, rolled down my window, and held up a rocket. I seriously thought the boys would see I was ready to take them to the park and just drop everything to come with me. They didn't. Conner just yelled, "We can go later on, we are playing right now Dad!"

That was the second time. Wow! I couldn't believe it. They were so excited to be able to launch these things and when it was finally time. They were not ready anymore. I'd be lying if I said I was not a bit disappointed we would not be able to do it. I just yelled back, "Ok guys, have fun, maybe later!" Then I just drove the rest of the way around the block to head home. I definitely was not "THE COOL KID" any longer.

As I was approaching the driveway, I seen both of them on their scooters heading home. I was really surprised to see them back so soon, but I was really happy. They got in the car with me and we headed to the park where we launched the rockets and I was able to teach them as much about science and wind as I could.

Sometimes I wonder if I have ever done anything like that to my dad to make him feel that way. I'll never know because, I know he will never say. I guess it might just be a Dad thing. We have to stay tough. The time we have with our kids is precious. I try my hardest to enjoy every day with them. I guess there is a reason people say we shouldn't be our kid's friends. Maybe it's because one day we wont be cool anymore and it's such a hard pill for us to swallow. I don't have to always be their friend. My kids will always know that no matter what, they will always have at least one friend, even if I am not always **"THE COOL KID."**

CHAPTER 12
Am I Prepared For Kids?

Ohhhhh the joys of having babies. All the new clothes you can buy for them. There is new furniture to buy, new toys to play with, and new shows to watch on television. Kids are really great, but do you know what they are not? They are not cheap. Kids are expensive. Just when we thought we had it all figured out with our first one, boom, here comes baby number two. Time for more new clothes. More new toys and more new furniture. We definitely thought we were ready for number two. She was way more ready than I was. Maybe because she has mother's instincts. I thought I was ready. I definitely had my mind made up I wanted children. That part was easy. We were both 100% ready for the babies. I just am not sure I realized how many diapers I'd change or how many sleepless nights I'd have. I am not sure how The Mama could do it. For every one sleepless night I had, she probably had fifty. There is no way I could ever be ready to change a poopy diaper too early and get a surprise shot all over my hand in the middle of changing it. There is no way I could have ever prepared myself for finding permanent marker on my freshly painted walls. There is no way I could have prepared myself for mold in my bathroom and a rotted floor from splashing in the bathtub, or sitting in pee countless times when waking up in the middle of the night to sneak to the bathroom. So, was I ready? Definitely yes! At least I thought I was anyway. Truth is, it's easy to be ready to love a baby. They are cute, sweet, and it's fun to kiss their chunky cheeks. Unless you end up with them turning their face and you get lips full of slobber. Even that's funny though, especially if it happens to someone else.

I know what you are thinking while reading this. "Which is it? Was he ready or not?" The answer is yes, I was ready to start a family. So, the question should be... Was I prepared?

Being prepared to have a baby and start a family is definitely a huge decision. I was totally ready for the new people we wanted to bring into this world, but I was not ready for some of the things that would happen after we had them. As parents we want to make sure our children are always safe and happy. We want to protect them at all cost. No matter how hard we try though, there are always those few factors in our perfect equation we either miss or get thrown at us when we least expect it.

I can remember folding laundry one morning while I was on the phone with Auntie Mandy. The Mama was on day shift at the time so she was working. Camden was barely able to sit on his own, so I had him propped up in the corner of the couch back and the arm. I had what seemed like twenty loads of laundry to fold. In reality it was probably only five or six; but who really enjoys folding laundry? Since Camden was so unstable, I put towels around him to keep him from falling forward. Or so I thought. Here I am trying to fold laundry, talk on the phone, and entertain a 5 month old all at the same time. I never have really been all that good at multitasking, I guess. I know I was on the phone, but he was right in front of me, so I don't think I was distracted. I looked away for a second to grab another piece of laundry to fold. Seriously a second maybe even less. Then it happened Camden rocked forward and BAM! He flipped right to the floor.

I instantly panicked I must have accidentally hung up on Auntie Mandy, when I picked him up right away. He was crying. I was screaming with tears flowing from my eyes. All I could do while checking him out was cry and pray he was ok. I was super scared he was hurt. Auntie Mandy must have called my dad or maybe I called him I am not really sure, but Camden stopped crying right away. I think he was more scared than hurt. My dad calmed me down in a few seconds. I totally forgot I had just hung up on Auntie Mandy. She was knocking on my door a few minutes later. She said she did not know what was going on so she decided to rush over.

Camden was completely fine. It would have made way more sense to let him play on the floor. I really am not sure why I'd sit him on the couch to be honest. I guess it proves my lack of experience with babies up until that point.

About a year later baby Conner was finally here. I remember driving him and The Mama home that hot day in late July. We arrived home and were checking out baby Conner watching him sleep. Camden was playing with his toys in his bedroom. All of a sudden, I look up and see him trying to walk on the window sill. Before I could even finish saying, "He is gonna fall!" Sure enough. BAM! There he went straight to the floor. His two little front teeth went right through his bottom lip and into his tongue. This kid is a bleeder there was a mess everywhere.

The Mama is a nurse so remember she sees blood every day. Blood from strangers, not her babies. This was her first hour home after having baby Conner. Her hormones and emotions were out of balance as it was. Now she has to deal with her baby who is bleeding all over the place. She was a wreck. She took care of him perfectly even with tears in her eyes.

She could not stop the bleeding and the cuts were all the way through his lip. She knew he had to go to the hospital. She was even more worked up because she couldn't take him. She had to stay home with Conner. We put Camden in his seat and gave him a cold wet rag to chew on. Then I put him in the car and back to the hospital I went. Again, I was super panicked about half way to the hospital I pulled over to check on him because he was really quiet. He was asleep! Here I am panicking and stressing out, and here he is asleep. I called my mother to tell her what was happening and both she and Aunt Lyssa met us at the emergency room. Today thinking back at it, I'm not sure why I drove him all the way to the same hospital we just left with Conner. There was another hospital about 15 minutes closer. When we arrived at the hospital Nana and Aunt Lyssa were already there. I am glad they came. I'm sure it helped Camden a lot seeing some familiar faces. The doctors seen him and just glued his cuts closed and said his tongue would heal fast.

Thankfully Camden let us learn from his ordeal, because he did it again about a year later and we were more prepared. This time though, he was running when he fell. I think he learned his lesson to not walk on the window sill.

We were going pretty good with our streak for not having to go to the hospital for a few years. I guess Camden was a little more careful and Conner was still too young, besides when we had the bumped head incident with Camden and an end table. That was stressful for me but his grandmas came to see him and said, "If the bump is indented it's bad and it's ok worry. If the bump comes out it will go down with ice and bruise, but he will be fine in about an hour." They were right it went exactly as they said. We did have some scraped knees, bumps, and bruises. All the wonderful joys of having boys. For the most part I'd say we were pretty lucky.

We were pretty lucky until Conner's day at the park. We live very close to a pretty large park. We take the boys there often to burn off some of their energy. We usually use it as a reward for them, but it is mostly a break for us I'd say at times. This place is great there are so many things to do. It's even fun for The Mama and I to run around and play with the guys. Sometimes there are a ton of kids. The boys always have a lot of fun.

The Mama took the boys one summer day while I was working to let them run off some energy after their dinner. There is a piece of equipment two kids can stand on at the same time and they can make spin around pretty fast using their arms. This piece of equipment is definitely not for any of us with a weak stomach, because it will cause us to get super dizzy super-fast. The boys were spinning, and before The Mama could grab Conner he had let go and bashed his forehead against it landing on the ground. It was probably a good thing The Mama was there since she is a nurse. She picked up Conner and quickly came home to clean his cut. After it was cleaned, she realized it was going to need stitches, so off to the hospital they went. On their way, The Mama called me. Her first words after I answered were, "He's ok, but Conner needs stitches in his head." She then explained to me what happened. I am super glad she started the conversation with "He's ok..." She knew I'd probably start stressing out if she just started with "Conner is headed to the hospital," or anything other than "He's ok..." What probably seems like common sense to start that way to tell someone, might not always be how it works out especially, in such a stressful situation. She has always been pretty good about keeping her cool in stressful situations.

Conner gave us all another pretty big scare on another warm summer evening as well. He was probably about 5 years old when it happened. Camden, Conner, The Mama, and myself were all outside waiting for someone to come over to remove some exercise equipment from our basement.

Both the boys were riding back and forth on the sidewalk with their scooters as they usually did almost every day. When the people finally arrived, we stood outside the garage talking about the two machines, work, and our kids. Everything was normal until we all heard Conner scream super loud.

Right away The Mama and I ran to him to see why he was screaming. We seen him fall off his scooter, but no one was sure why he was so upset. That is, until we came a bit closer. Right away The Mama scooped him into her arms and ran him into the house. Again, there was blood everywhere. This time there was a pool of blood on the sidewalk, his scooter, and all over his shirt. He had busted his mouth on the handlebars somehow.

Our guess was he hit an uneven spot in the sidewalk he was not ready for. He was not very tall at the time so the handlebars were about the same height as his mouth. When she brought him in the house right away, she took him to the bathroom sink to rinse his mouth. She told him not to look at the mirror, of course, we all know it's the first thing he did. He did not seem anymore scared than he already was though.

His top tooth was knocked loose and he had a pretty deep gash on his upper gum. We had to arrange for a pickup of the exercise equipment for a different day, because we were now taking another unexpected trip to the emergency room. The doctors looked at his mouth and decided to not do any x-rays because of his age. The bleeding had stopped from his wash rag we were using to apply pressure. We were told to follow up with the dentist the next day.

We called our dentist's emergency phone number as soon as we came home. Since the hospital sent us home already, she asked if we could send her pictures. After she seen them, she told us to come in first thing in the morning.

The next day the dentist took a few x-rays and told us his tooth would probably turn gray, because the nerves were damaged. She showed the x-rays to us and we could see his adult teeth were not damaged thankfully. She called his tooth a dead tooth. She also told us he should have had stitches in his gum, but it was too late for her to do them. I guess we only had a couple hours after he cut it to have them done.

She was right about the tooth. It was definitely dead. Not even a month later, it did turn gray. He hated his gray tooth every day until it was gone. It stayed loose for almost a year until the dentist had to finally remove it. Today you would not even know it happened unless he told you.

Kids are amazing. They are fun to be around and easy to love. They do scare us at times and can be pretty expensive, but are worth every mini heart attack and penny.

So, I'll say it again: "Yes, I was definitely 100% ready to have babies and kids." However, I could have never been prepared to see them get hurt. They will always keep you on your toes. When you think you have it all figured out you can scratch that idea. There will always be a cut to bandage or a bruise to ice.

For every hospital visit and every copay. There will be way more smiles and hugs. Babies are easy compared to kids sometimes, and sometimes the other way around. After you are ready to have babies, remember to ask yourself... **AM I PREPARED FOR KIDS?**

GEORGE'S THOUGHTS

It's not always easy being a Dad. There are going to be times no matter how hard we try we wont be able to take the smile off of our faces. There are most definitely going to be times we just want to pull our hair out or scream at the top of our lungs. There will even be times we will be more scared or tired than we ever thought possible.

While teaching our kids, we will learn more from them than we'd ever expect as well. It definitely goes both ways. I am learning new things everyday from my guys. Time is short and they grow up so fast.

I pray, I can always be there when they need me, even when we are not on the same schedule as they get older. I want them to remember what they have learned from me for situations when I am not around to guide them. I know I will not always physically be by their side, but I want to always be in their hearts. When times get tough I hope they can ask themselves, "What would Daddy do?"

Part 2 Preview

BOY DAD

PART 2
A Collection Of Fond Memories

Having Leftovers

Isn't it nice to be able to wake up and make a fresh warm breakfast? How about, coming in from a long day and eating a fresh hot dinner? Even better yet, how about, going to a restaurant and getting something freshly made for you? It's so great. It really is a wonderful thing to eat something freshly made. Honestly, I never realized how great a hot meal actually was, until I had children.

At home, right after the meal was made, we would have to make a plate for the kids. We would have everything cut up and make sure they ate. We would then, have to clean up after them and wash all the dishes. Sure, we would be hungry, but when you have 2 little guys to take care of it was just something that had to get done. I would say, I finally figured it out after Camden was maybe 3 years old.

Not every meal was always cold, of course, there were many times when they would eat at different times or we would eat during their nap time. It was always wonderful to attend a family function with food, because someone always wanted the baby. What a relief it is to have family, usually it's almost as if, we have about 5 sitters and we are there with them. Thanksgiving, Christmas, Easter, any holiday really, were always great too, because I could eat as much as I wanted and still fall asleep afterward without worrying about the kids.

So, there are a lot of times we did get hot meals when they were babies, but there are a ton of times you do not get one at all. Even if it is hot, you don't get to relax. I'd always be either trying to feed them or cleaning up their messes at the same time. For some reason everything on my plate seemed to look tastier to them too, so The Dada was always sharing his plate it seemed. Even though, we were eating the same exact thing.

There were so many times we would end up eating cold meals, we would not even put anything in the microwave anymore. Cold chicken, cold mac and cheese, even soup we would eat cold. Picking up fast food was great, we could eat that in the car. Since having Cohen, so far, I have not had the cold meal problem too many times, yet. Maybe, taking care of 1 baby is a lot easier, or maybe I finally figured it out.

Cold meals might not be a great perk as a result of having kids, but do you know what is? Left overs! Until I was living on my own or with just me and The Mama, never have I been happy about left overs. Everything changes when you have to pay for it yourself, I guess. Left overs are so great it's almost like "Buy one get one free!"

If cold meals and left overs were not enough. How about late dinners? How about really late? During summer time, it does not seem so bad to have dinner at about 8 p.m. The sun is usually still out or just going down. The kids are probably still outside playing too. Life is already busy as it is before kids. Throw three of them in the mix and you will see, life before kids was a vacation. Being super busy all day long and eating dinner late in the summer is one thing. How about winter? They do have school in the morning. Sometimes we do not even start dinner until 7:30 or so. Most of the time it's a normal thing. The only bad things I can think of about having a late dinner is: the snack drawer empties fast, we can't burn off the calories before bed, and depending how busy the kid's days were, they might fall asleep before its ready. I am guilty of waiting too long sometimes to make dinner. I have even been too tired to make anything at all and just ask the kids if they want cereal for dinner. They love it. Normally cereal is just breakfast, so they get super excited. They are excited and I am relieved, because they are not going to bed hungry and I can relax when I'm super tired.

There are so many times The Mama or myself make too much food. We would rather have too much than not enough. I work afternoon shift. Sometimes when I get home the kid's plates are still at the table. It is not always a great thing when they do not eat everything on their plates, but after a long day of work, I'm usually pretty hungry. Whatever they don't eat I get to add to my plate. In case you didn't already know, I usually am a pretty big eater. One day it will catch up to me I am sure. Hopefully, not anytime soon though. Left overs are always great for the next day too. It's so nice to have something already prepared, especially after a long day.

Sometimes, as a new parent we might have cold meals and they seem to be normal. Sharing our plate even though we have the same thing is normal too. I still cannot remember the last time I was able to eat my own pickle with a hamburger from a restaurant. Wasted food is something we see regularly as well. It is not always a bad thing. Kids will always eat when they are hungry. Just because they don't eat it might not mean, they don't like the food. I'll say it again, "Its sometimes nice to have something already prepared from the previous day in the fridge." That is, if The Dada has not already eaten it. If not, a late dinner is always better than no dinner, especially when we are all hungry. The next time someone ask, "what's for dinner?" Remember, the good reasons, for **"HAVING LEFTOVERS."**

AFTER YOU!

We always want what is best for our children. We always want them to be able to make good decisions and the right choices. We want them to grow up with good manners and have respect for everyone and animals. How will we do it? How is it even possible? We are always so busy with errands, housework, and preparing and cooking meals. We can't forget to mention their sports or other after school activities. How is it possible to even find the time?

This part of parenting in my opinion is the easiest. I don't have answers to every question in the world, even though my boys might think I do. Let's face it, when The Mama asks me a question I have a hard time answering it's easy to answer that one too. I just tell her, "I'm not very good with Trivia!" That one might not always be the best answer and I feel like I should add a disclosure to that one. "DO NOT TRY THAT AT HOME!"

All joking aside though. The reason I think this part of parenting is the easiest is because you don't have to teach it at all. You have to just do it! Kids are always watching everything. They are always learning. They see and know way more than we think, so it's important us parents lead by example. So, there is the answer.

Don't just tell them how you want them to act. SHOW THEM! Teach them it's ok to not always win and teach them to be happy for the other guy. Let them see you open the door for women, the elderly, or someone who is at the door the same time. Show them how to react when something does not always go as planned, by keeping your cool. Let them see you being polite to everyone and being gentle to animals.

They look up to us. They will take all the things we do and decide what pieces they keep to make them who they will become as adults. They represent us and who we are as parents.

Sure, they are kids and they are going to make tons of bad decisions. They will make tons of good ones too. I want our boys to grow up to be great men one day. I want people to be able to say their names and smile. So, am I doing it right? I hope so.

Every time I go anywhere whether it be alone or with my guys. I am always the one to hold the door for someone or let them be first in line. When I am with the boys, I always make sure to tell them to either, "Hold the door" or "Hold the door for the lady." These words I know my boys have heard countless times. I witness them doing it now every time. The Mama and I have definitely created a good habit for them.

It was winter. The three boys and myself had to wake up early so Camden could get to school early for running club. On this particular day it was really cold outside. We live in Michigan, so our winters can be pretty cold. On this particular morning the temperature was less than 20°F. The wind was blowing pretty hard too. Camden was dressed appropriately for the weather of course. There is no doubt the wind was really cold on him though.

I always watch him walk in and I stay until the door closes behind him. He usually walks in right away and heads straight to where he has to be. Not this time though. This time he noticed something before I did. He seen a woman getting ready to cross the parking lot with a box in her hands. He waited! Even though the temperature was less than 20°F and the wind was blowing really strong. He waited! He stood outside the door and waited until she was close so he could hold the door for her.

It could have been 20 below that day and as much as I hate the cold I probably would not have even cared at that moment. It warmed my heart to see my boy not just hold the door for someone, but to put someone else's comfort before his own. The smile on my face that morning could have lit up the darkest of nights. This was definitely a proud Daddy moment for me.

Sometimes moments like these seem as if they should just always play out that way. Unfortunately, we all know it is not always the case. Sure, this is just one example. He probably did not even know I was watching. I am positive his small good deed did not go unnoticed, especially for the women with the box. So, the next time we think, "how do we know for sure our kids are making the right choices or being respectful?" We can just ask ourselves, "Are we leading by good example?" Can we be positive that our children will always say, **<u>"AFTER YOU!"</u>**

More books by this author:
BOY DAD,
Short memoirs from a father of young boys
BOY DAD pt.2,
A collection of fond memories
BEHIND CLOSED DOORS,
If walls could talk (*coming soon, late 2020*)

Don't miss out!

Visit the website below and you can sign up to receive emails whenever G.T. DIGUE publishes a new book. There's no charge and no obligation.

https://books2read.com/r/B-A-JMOK-NLEFB

BOOKS 2 READ

Connecting independent readers to independent writers.

www.ingramcontent.com/pod-product-compliance
Lightning Source LLC
Chambersburg PA
CBHW071837020426
42331CB00007B/1759